HAL•LEONARD

JAZZ PLAY ALONG®

Book and CD for B♭, E♭ and C Instruments

volume
64

TV Tunes

10 favorite television themes

Arranged by
Mark Taylor and Jim Roberts

Produced by Paul Murtha

Book

CD

TITLE	PAGE NUMBERS			
	C Treble Instruments	B♭ Instruments	E♭ Instruments	C Bass Instruments
Bandstand Boogie	4	18	32	46
Theme from Family Guy	6	20	34	48
Theme from "Frasier"	7	21	35	49
Hawaii Five-O Theme	8	22	36	50
Love and Marriage	10	24	38	52
Mission: Impossible Theme	9	23	37	51
The Odd Couple	12	26	40	54
Theme from The Simpsons™	14	28	42	56
Theme from Spider Man	16	30	44	58
Theme from "Star Trek®"	13	27	41	55

TITLE	CD Track Number Split Track / Melody	CD Track Number Full Stereo Track
Bandstand Boogie	1	2
Theme from Family Guy	3	4
Theme from "Frasier"	5	6
Hawaii Five-O Theme	7	8
Love and Marriage	9	10
Mission: Impossible Theme	11	12
The Odd Couple	13	14
Theme from The Simpsons™	15	16
Theme from Spider Man	17	18
Theme from "Star Trek®"	19	20
B♭ Tuning Notes		21

ISBN-13: 978-1-4234-1342-4
ISBN-10: 1-4234-1342-3

T0083922

HAL•LEONARD®
CORPORATION

7777 W. BLUEMOUND RD. P.O. BOX 13819 MILWAUKEE, WI 53213

Visit Hal Leonard Online at
www.halleonard.com

TV Tunes

Volume 64

Arranged by Mark Taylor and Jim Roberts
Produced by Paul Murtha

Featured Players:

Graham Breedlove–Trumpet
John Desalme–Saxophones
Tony Nalker–Piano
Jim Roberts–Bass
Steve Fidyk–Drums

HOW TO USE THE CD:

Each song has <u>two</u> tracks:

1) Split Track/Melody

Woodwind, Brass, Keyboard, and **Mallet Players** can use this track as a learning tool for melody style and inflection.

Bass Players can learn and perform with this track – remove the recorded bass track by turning down the volume on the LEFT channel.

Keyboard and **Guitar Players** can learn and perform with this track – remove the recorded piano part by turning down the volume on the RIGHT channel.

2) Full Stereo Track

Soloists or **Groups** can learn and perform with this accompaniment track with the RHYTHM SECTION only.

BANDSTAND BOOGIE
FROM THE TELEVISION SERIES AMERICAN BANDSTAND

C VERSION

SPECIAL LYRIC BY BARRY MANILOW AND BRUCE SUSSMAN
MUSIC BY CHARLES ALBERTINE

SOLO

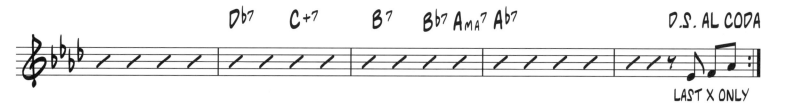

D.S. AL CODA

LAST X ONLY

CD

3 : SPLIT TRACK/MELODY
4 : FULL STEREO TRACK

C VERSION

THEME FROM FAMILY GUY
FROM THE TWENTIETH CENTURY FOX TELEVISION SERIES FAMILY GUY

WORDS BY SETH MACFARLANE AND DAVID ZUCKERMAN
MUSIC BY WALTER MURPHY

CD
◆5 : SPLIT TRACK/MELODY
◆6 : FULL STEREO TRACK

C VERSION

THEME FROM "FRASIER"
FROM THE PARAMOUNT TELEVISION SERIES FRASIER

WORDS BY DARRYL PHINNESSEE
MUSIC BY BRUCE MILLER

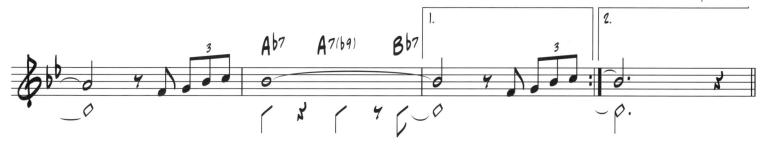

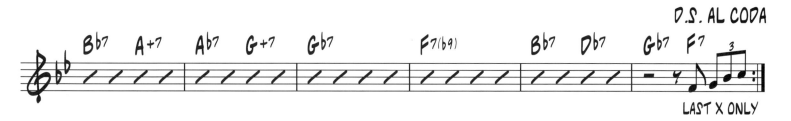

HAWAII FIVE-O THEME

FROM THE TELEVISION SERIES

BY MORT STEVENS

MISSION: IMPOSSIBLE THEME
FROM THE PARAMOUNT TELEVISION SERIES MISSION: IMPOSSIBLE

BY LALO SCHIFRIN

C VERSION

CD

◆ 9 : SPLIT TRACK/MELODY
◆ 10 : FULL STEREO TRACK

C VERSION

LOVE AND MARRIAGE

FROM THE TELEVISION SERIES MARRIED ... WITH CHILDREN

WORDS BY SAMMY CAHN
MUSIC BY JAMES VAN HEUSEN

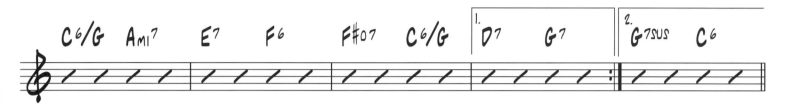

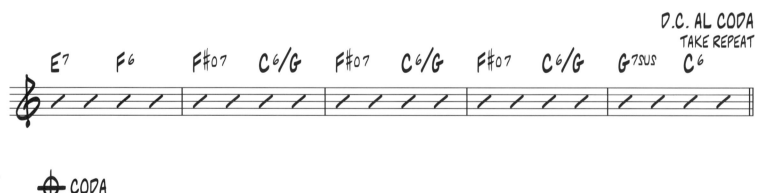

CD
- **13** : SPLIT TRACK/MELODY
- **14** : FULL STEREO TRACK

THE ODD COUPLE
THEME FROM THE PARAMOUNT TELEVISION SERIES THE ODD COUPLE

BY NEAL HEFTI

C VERSION

Theme from "Star Trek"®

FROM THE PARAMOUNT TELEVISION SERIES STAR TREK

WORDS BY GENE RODDENBERRY
MUSIC BY ALEXANDER COURAGE

C VERSION

CD

15 : SPLIT TRACK/MELODY
16 : FULL STEREO TRACK

THEME FROM THE SIMPSON'S™
FROM THE TWENTIETH CENTURY FOX TELEVISION SERIES THE SIMPSONS™

C VERSION

MUSIC BY DANNY ELFMAN

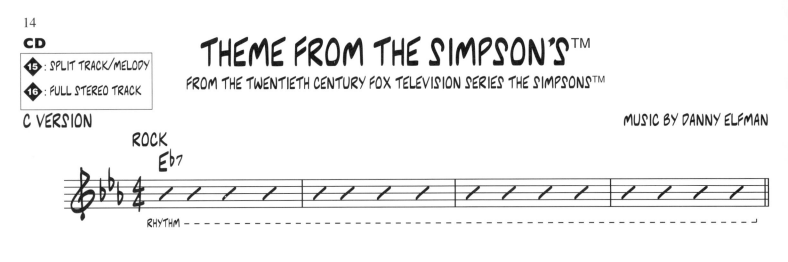

TO CODA ⊕

SOLOS (4 CHORUSES)

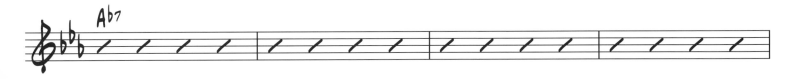

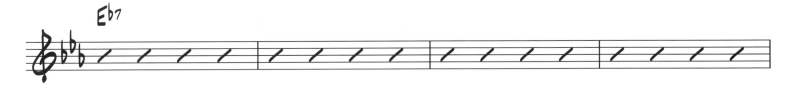

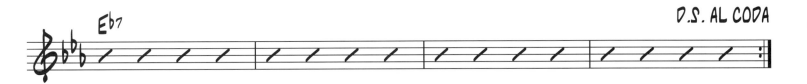

THEME FROM SPIDER MAN

CD

17: SPLIT TRACK/MELODY

18: FULL STEREO TRACK

WRITTEN BY BOB HARRIS
AND PAUL FRANCIS WEBSTER

C VERSION

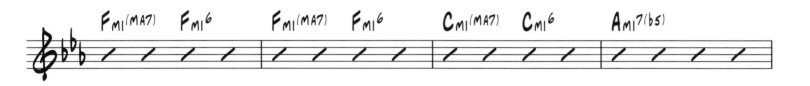

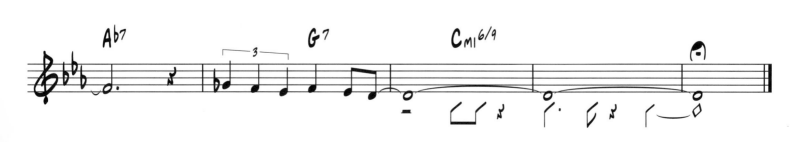

BANDSTAND BOOGIE
FROM THE TELEVISION SERIES AMERICAN BANDSTAND

SPECIAL LYRIC BY BARRY MANILOW AND BRUCE SUSSMAN
MUSIC BY CHARLES ALBERTINE

Bb Version

SOLO

D.S. AL CODA

LAST X ONLY

CODA

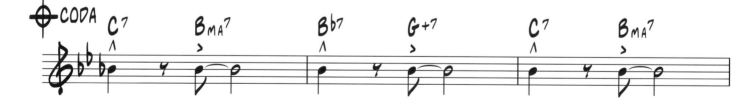

THEME FROM FAMILY GUY

FROM THE TWENTIETH CENTURY FOX TELEVISION SERIES FAMILY GUY

WORDS BY SETH MACFARLANE AND DAVID ZUCKERMAN
MUSIC BY WALTER MURPHY

THEME FROM "FRASIER"
FROM THE PARAMOUNT TELEVISION SERIES FRASIER

WORDS BY DARRYL PHINNESSEE
MUSIC BY BRUCE MILLER

CD
5 : SPLIT TRACK/MELODY
6 : FULL STEREO TRACK

B♭ VERSION

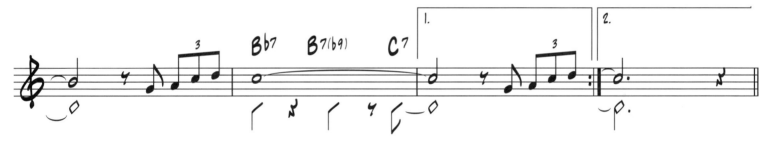

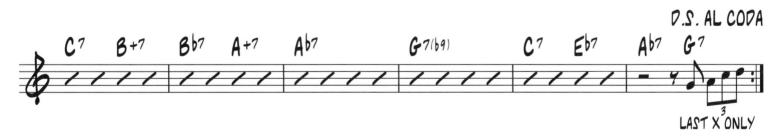

HAWAII FIVE-O THEME

FROM THE TELEVISION SERIES

BY MORT STEVENS

MISSION: IMPOSSIBLE THEME
FROM THE PARAMOUNT TELEVISION SERIES MISSION: IMPOSSIBLE

BY LALO SCHIFRIN

LOVE AND MARRIAGE

FROM THE TELEVISION SERIES MARRIED ... WITH CHILDREN

WORDS BY SAMMY CAHN
MUSIC BY JAMES VAN HEUSEN

CD
9 : SPLIT TRACK/MELODY
10 : FULL STEREO TRACK

Bb Version

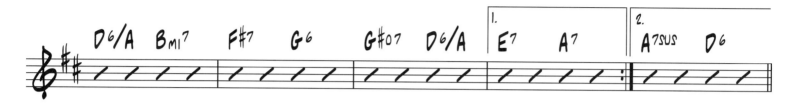

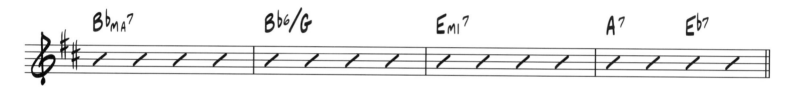

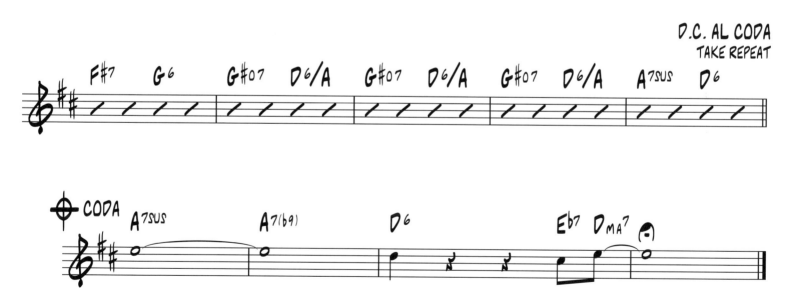

THE ODD COUPLE
THEME FROM THE PARAMOUNT TELEVISION SERIES THE ODD COUPLE

BY NEAL HEFTI

THEME FROM "STAR TREK®"
FROM THE PARAMOUNT TELEVISION SERIES STAR TREK

WORDS BY GENE RODDENBERRY
MUSIC BY ALEXANDER COURAGE

Bb VERSION

Theme from The Simpson's™

From the Twentieth Century Fox Television Series The Simpsons™

Music by Danny Elfman

Bb Version

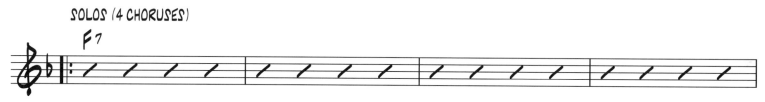

SOLOS (4 CHORUSES)

F7

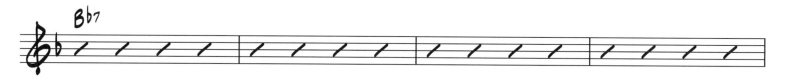

Bb7

F7

C7   Bb7

D.S. AL CODA

F7

CODA

C7   Bb7

F7   E7/F   F6

CD

THEME FROM SPIDER MAN

WRITTEN BY BOB HARRIS
AND PAUL FRANCIS WEBSTER

B♭ VERSION

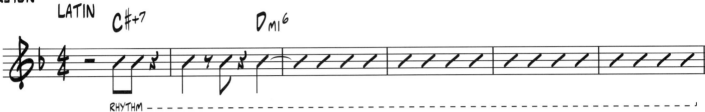

CD

1 : SPLIT TRACK/MELODY
2 : FULL STEREO TRACK

BANDSTAND BOOGIE
FROM THE TELEVISION SERIES AMERICAN BANDSTAND

SPECIAL LYRIC BY BARRY MANILOW AND BRUCE SUSSMAN
MUSIC BY CHARLES ALBERTINE

Eb VERSION

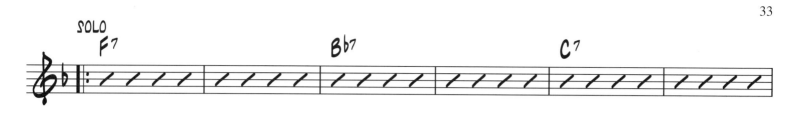

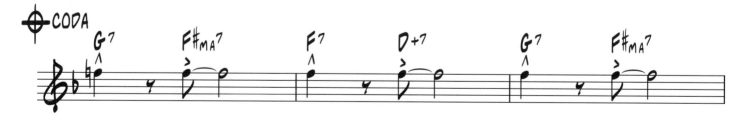

THEME FROM FAMILY GUY

FROM THE TWENTIETH CENTURY FOX TELEVISION SERIES FAMILY GUY

WORDS BY SETH MACFARLANE AND DAVID ZUCKERMAN
MUSIC BY WALTER MURPHY

Theme From "Frasier"
FROM THE PARAMOUNT TELEVISION SERIES FRASIER

WORDS BY DARRYL PHINNESSEE
MUSIC BY BRUCE MILLER

E♭ VERSION

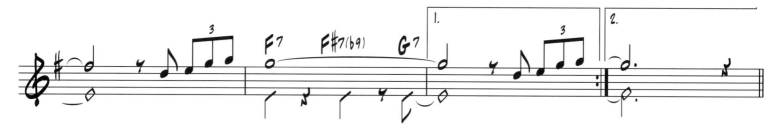

HAWAII FIVE-O THEME

FROM THE TELEVISION SERIES

BY MORT STEVENS

MISSION: IMPOSSIBLE THEME
FROM THE PARAMOUNT TELEVISION SERIES MISSION: IMPOSSIBLE

BY LALO SCHIFRIN

CD
11 : SPLIT TRACK/MELODY
12 : FULL STEREO TRACK

Eb VERSION

LOVE AND MARRIAGE

FROM THE TELEVISION SERIES MARRIED ... WITH CHILDREN

WORDS BY SAMMY CAHN
MUSIC BY JAMES VAN HEUSEN

CD
- **9** : SPLIT TRACK/MELODY
- **10** : FULL STEREO TRACK

Eb VERSION

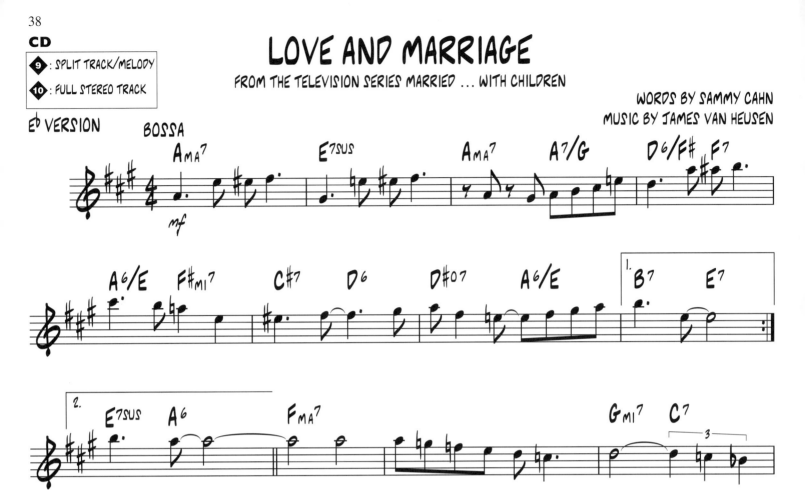

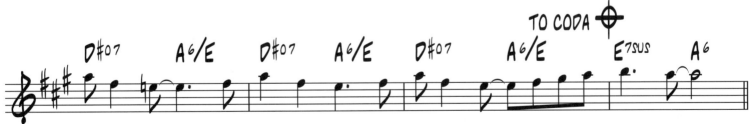

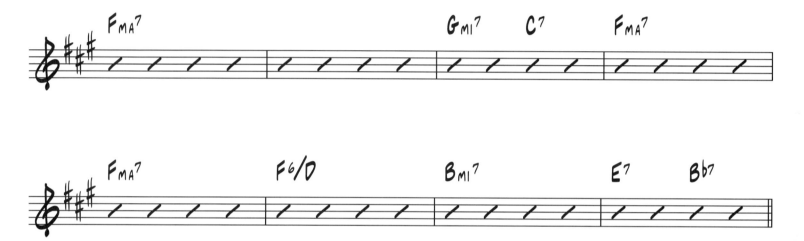

THE ODD COUPLE

THEME FROM THE PARAMOUNT TELEVISION SERIES THE ODD COUPLE

BY NEAL HEFTI

THEME FROM "STAR TREK®"

FROM THE PARAMOUNT TELEVISION SERIES STAR TREK

WORDS BY GENE RODDENBERRY
MUSIC BY ALEXANDER COURAGE

THEME FROM THE SIMPSON'S™
FROM THE TWENTIETH CENTURY FOX TELEVISION SERIES THE SIMPSONS™

MUSIC BY DANNY ELFMAN

CD
15 : SPLIT TRACK/MELODY
16 : FULL STEREO TRACK

E♭ VERSION

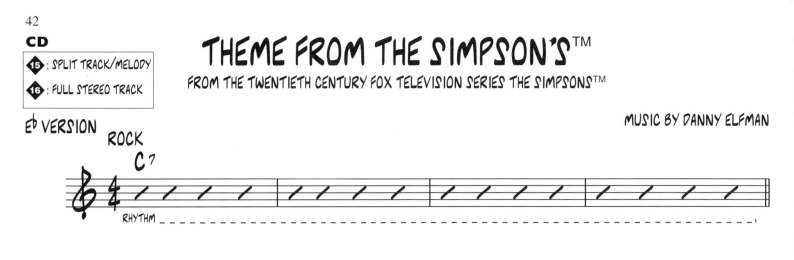

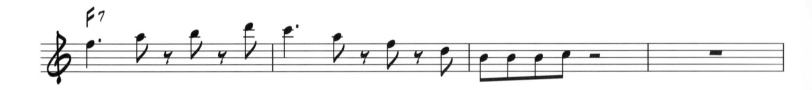

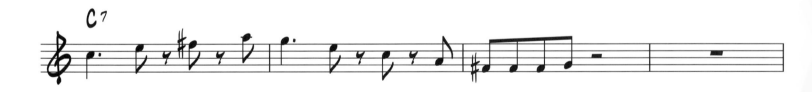

SOLOS (4 CHORUSES)

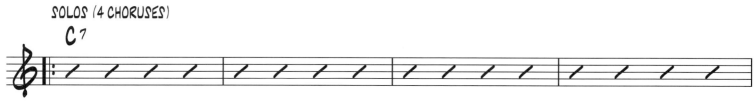

D.S. AL CODA

CODA

CD

THEME FROM SPIDER MAN

WRITTEN BY BOB HARRIS
AND PAUL FRANCIS WEBSTER

E♭ VERSION

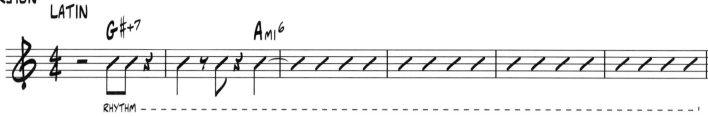

CD

◆ 1 : SPLIT TRACK/MELODY

◆ 2 : FULL STEREO TRACK

BANDSTAND BOOGIE
FROM THE TELEVISION SERIES AMERICAN BANDSTAND

SPECIAL LYRIC BY BARRY MANILOW AND BRUCE SUSSMAN
MUSIC BY CHARLES ALBERTINE

𝄢: C VERSION

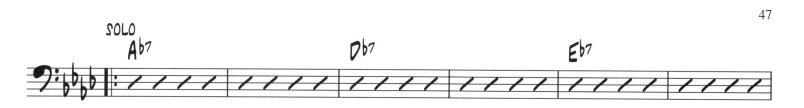

THEME FROM FAMILY GUY

FROM THE TWENTIETH CENTURY FOX TELEVISION SERIES FAMILY GUY

WORDS BY SETH MACFARLANE AND DAVID ZUCKERMAN
MUSIC BY WALTER MURPHY

Theme From "Frasier"

FROM THE PARAMOUNT TELEVISION SERIES FRASIER

WORDS BY DARRYL PHINNESSEE
MUSIC BY BRUCE MILLER

𝄢: C VERSION

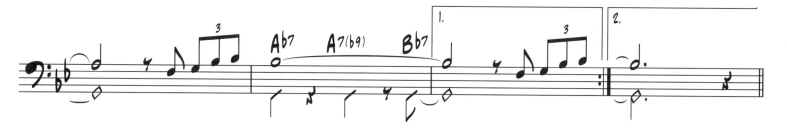

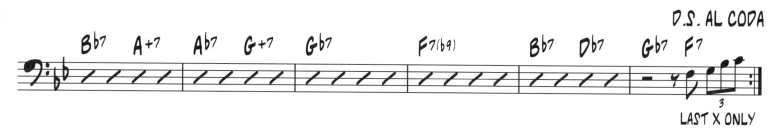

HAWAII FIVE-O THEME
FROM THE TELEVISION SERIES

BY MORT STEVENS

MISSION: IMPOSSIBLE THEME
FROM THE PARAMOUNT TELEVISION SERIES MISSION: IMPOSSIBLE

BY LALO SCHIFRIN

LOVE AND MARRIAGE

FROM THE TELEVISION SERIES MARRIED ... WITH CHILDREN

WORDS BY SAMMY CAHN
MUSIC BY JAMES VAN HEUSEN

: C VERSION

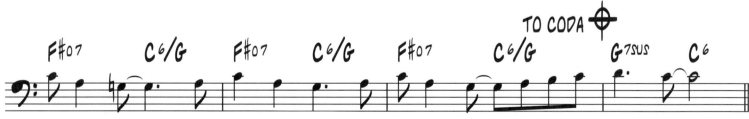

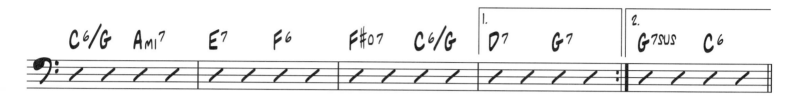

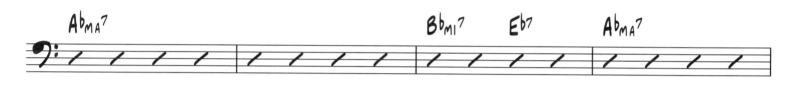

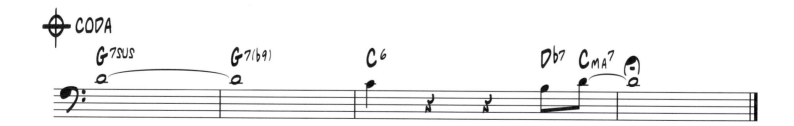

CD

13 : SPLIT TRACK/MELODY
14 : FULL STEREO TRACK

THE ODD COUPLE
THEME FROM THE PARAMOUNT TELEVISION SERIES THE ODD COUPLE

BY NEAL HEFTI

Theme from "Star Trek"
FROM THE PARAMOUNT TELEVISION SERIES STAR TREK

WORDS BY GENE RODDENBERRY
MUSIC BY ALEXANDER COURAGE

CD
15 : SPLIT TRACK/MELODY
16 : FULL STEREO TRACK

THEME FROM THE SIMPSON'S™

FROM THE TWENTIETH CENTURY FOX TELEVISION SERIES THE SIMPSONS™

MUSIC BY DANNY ELFMAN

𝄢 : C VERSION

ROCK

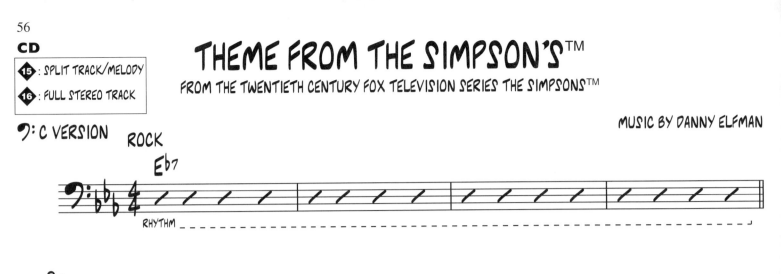

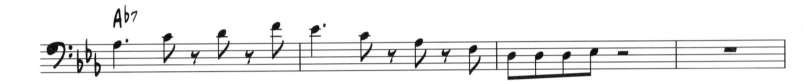

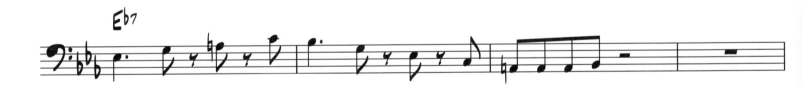

TO CODA ⊕

SOLOS (4 CHORUSES)

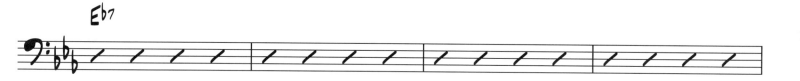

THEME FROM SPIDER MAN

WRITTEN BY BOB HARRIS
AND PAUL FRANCIS WEBSTER

CD
17 : SPLIT TRACK/MELODY
18 : FULL STEREO TRACK

𝄢: C VERSION

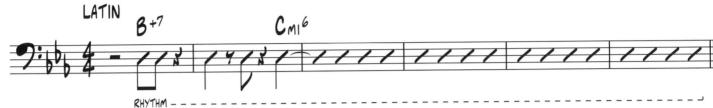

Jazz Instruction & Improvisation
Books for All Instruments from Hal Leonard

AN APPROACH TO JAZZ IMPROVISATION
by Dave Pozzi
Musicians Institute Press
Explore the styles of Charlie Parker, Sonny Rollins, Bud Powell and others with this comprehensive guide to jazz improvisation. Covers: scale choices • chord analysis • phrasing • melodies • harmonic progressions • more.
00695135 Book/CD Pack $17.95

BUILDING A JAZZ VOCABULARY
By Mike Steinel
A valuable resource for learning the basics of jazz from Mike Steinel of the University of North Texas. It covers: the basics of jazz • how to build effective solos • a comprehensive practice routine • and a jazz vocabulary of the masters.
00849911 ....$19.95

THE CYCLE OF FIFTHS
by Emile and Laura De Cosmo
This essential instruction book provides more than 450 exercises, including hundreds of melodic and rhythmic ideas. The book is designed to help improvisors master the cycle of fifths, one of the primary progressions in music. Guaranteed to refine technique, enhance improvisational fluency, and improve sight-reading!
00311114 ....$14.95

THE DIATONIC CYCLE
by Emile and Laura De Cosmo
Renowned jazz educators Emile and Laura De Cosmo provide more than 300 exercises to help improvisors tackle one of music's most common progressions: the diatonic cycle. This book is guaranteed to refine technique, enhance improvisational fluency, and improve sight-reading!
00311115 ....$16.95

EAR TRAINING
by Keith Wyatt, Carl Schroeder and Joe Elliott
Musicians Institute Press
Covers: basic pitch matching • singing major and minor scales • identifying intervals • transcribing melodies and rhythm • identifying chords and progressions • seventh chords and the blues • modal interchange, chromaticism, modulation • and more.
00695198 Book/2-CD Pack....................$19.95

EXERCISES AND ETUDES FOR THE JAZZ INSTRUMENTALIST
by J.J. Johnson
Designed as study material and playable by any instrument, these pieces run the gamut of the jazz experience, featuring common and uncommon time signatures and keys, and styles from ballads to funk. They are progressively graded so that both beginners and professionals will be challenged by the demands of this wonderful music.
00842018 Bass Clef Edition....................................$16.95
00842042 Treble Clef Edition $16.95

JAZZOLOGY
THE ENCYCLOPEDIA OF JAZZ THEORY FOR ALL MUSICIANS
by Robert Rawlins and Nor Eddine Bahha
This comprehensive resource covers a variety of jazz topics, for beginners and pros of any instrument. The book serves as an encyclopedia for reference, a thorough methodology for the student, and a workbook for the classroom.
00311167 ....$17.95

JAZZ THEORY RESOURCES
by Bert Ligon
Houston Publishing, Inc.
This is a jazz theory text in two volumes. **Volume 1 includes:** review of basic theory • rhythm in jazz performance • triadic generalization • diatonic harmonic progressions and analysis • substitutions and turnarounds • and more. **Volume 2 includes:** modes and modal frameworks • quartal harmony • extended tertian structures and triadic superimposition • pentatonic applications • coloring "outside" the lines and beyond • and more.
00030458 Volume 1 ....$39.95
00030459 Volume 2 ....$29.95

JOY OF IMPROV
by Dave Frank and John Amaral
This book/CD course on improvisation for all instruments and all styles will help players develop monster musical skills! **Book One** imparts a solid basis in technique, rhythm, chord theory, ear training and improv concepts. **Book Two** explores more advanced chord voicings, chord arranging techniques and more challenging blues and melodic lines. The CD can be used as a listening and play-along tool.
00220005 Book 1 – Book/CD Pack $24.95
00220006 Book 2 – Book/CD Pack $24.95

THE PATH TO JAZZ IMPROVISATION
by Emile and Laura De Cosmo
This fascinating jazz instruction book offers an innovative, scholarly approach to the art of improvisation. It includes in-depth analysis and lessons about: cycle of fifths • diatonic cycle • overtone series • pentatonic scale • harmonic and melodic minor scale • polytonal order of keys • blues and bebop scales • modes • and more.
00310904 ....$14.95

THE SOURCE
THE DICTIONARY OF CONTEMPORARY AND TRADITIONAL SCALES
by Steve Barta
This book serves as an informative guide for people who are looking for good, solid information regarding scales, chords, and how they work together. It provides right and left hand fingerings for scales, chords, and complete inversions. Includes over 20 different scales, each written in all 12 keys.
00240885 ....$12.95

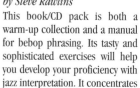

21 BEBOP EXERCISES
by Steve Rawlins
This book/CD pack is both a warm-up collection and a manual for bebop phrasing. Its tasty and sophisticated exercises will help you develop your proficiency with jazz interpretation. It concentrates on practice in all twelve keys – moving higher by half-step – to help develop dexterity and range. The companion CD includes all of the exercises in 12 keys.
00315341 Book/CD Pack $17.95

THE WOODSHEDDING SOURCE BOOK
by Emile De Cosmo
Rehearsing with this method daily will improve technique, reading ability, rhythmic and harmonic vocabulary, eye/finger coordination, endurance, range, theoretical knowledge, and listening skills – all of which lead to superior improvisational skills.
00842000 C Instruments $19.95

FOR MORE INFORMATION, SEE YOUR LOCAL MUSIC DEALER, OR WRITE TO:

HAL•LEONARD® CORPORATION
7777 W. BLUEMOUND RD. P.O. BOX 13819 MILWAUKEE, WI 53213

Prices, contents & availability subject to change without notice.

Visit Hal Leonard online at
www.halleonard.com

ARTIST TRANSCRIPTIONS

Artist Transcriptions are authentic, note-for-note transcriptions of today's hottest artists in jazz, pop and rock. These outstanding, accurate arrangements are in an easy-to-read format which includes all essential lines. Artist Transcriptions can be used to perform, sequence or for reference.

CLARINET

00672423	Buddy De Franco Collection	$19.95

FLUTE

00672379	Eric Dolphy Collection	$19.95
00672372	James Moody Collection – Sax and Flute	$19.95
00660108	James Newton – Improvising Flute	$14.95
00672455	Lew Tabackin Collection	$19.95

GUITAR & BASS

00660113	The Guitar Style of George Benson	$14.95
00672331	Ron Carter – Acoustic Bass	$16.95
00660115	Al Di Meola – Friday Night in San Francisco	$14.95
00604043	Al Di Meola – Music, Words, Pictures	$14.95
00673245	Jazz Style of Tal Farlow	$19.95
00672359	Bela Fleck and the Flecktones	$18.95
00699389	Jim Hall – Jazz Guitar Environments	$19.95
00699306	Jim Hall – Exploring Jazz Guitar	$19.95
00672335	Best of Scott Henderson	$24.95
00672356	Jazz Guitar Standards	$19.95
00675536	Wes Montgomery – Guitar Transcriptions	$17.95
00672353	Joe Pass Collection	$18.95
00673216	John Patitucci	$16.95
00672374	Johnny Smith Guitar Solos	$16.95
00672320	Mark Whitfield	$19.95
00672337	Gary Willis Collection	$19.95

PIANO & KEYBOARD

00672338	Monty Alexander Collection	$19.95
00672487	Monty Alexander Plays Standards	$19.95
00672318	Kenny Barron Collection	$22.95
00672520	Count Basie Collection	$19.95
00672364	Warren Bernhardt Collection	$19.95
00672439	Cyrus Chestnut Collection	$19.95
00673242	Billy Childs Collection	$19.95
00672300	Chick Corea – Paint the World	$12.95
00672537	Bill Evans at Town Hall	$16.95
00672425	Bill Evans – Piano Interpretations	$19.95
00672365	Bill Evans – Piano Standards	$19.95
00672510	Bill Evans Trio – Vol. 1: 1959-1961	$24.95
00672511	Bill Evans Trio – Vol. 2: 1962-1965	$24.95
00672512	Bill Evans Trio – Vol. 3: 1968-1974	$24.95
00672513	Bill Evans Trio – Vol. 4: 1979-1980	$24.95
00672329	Benny Green Collection	$19.95
00672486	Vince Guaraldi Collection	$19.95
00672419	Herbie Hancock Collection	$19.95
00672446	Gene Harris Collection	$19.95
00672438	Hampton Hawes	$19.95
00672322	Ahmad Jamal Collection	$22.95
00672476	Brad Mehldau Collection	$19.95

00672390	Thelonious Monk Plays Jazz Standards – Volume 1	$19.95
00672391	Thelonious Monk Plays Jazz Standards – Volume 2	$19.95
00672433	Jelly Roll Morton – The Piano Rolls	$12.95
00672542	Oscar Peterson – Jazz Piano Solos	$14.95
00672544	Oscar Peterson – Originals	$9.95
00672532	Oscar Peterson – Plays Broadway	$19.95
00672531	Oscar Peterson – Plays Duke Ellington	$19.95
00672533	Oscar Peterson – Trios	$24.95
00672543	Oscar Peterson Trio – Canadiana Suite	$7.95
00672534	Very Best of Oscar Peterson	$22.95
00672371	Bud Powell Classics	$19.95
00672376	Bud Powell Collection	$19.95
00672437	André Previn Collection	$19.95
00672507	Gonzalo Rubalcaba Collection	$19.95
00672303	Horace Silver Collection	$19.95
00672316	Art Tatum Collection	$22.95
00672355	Art Tatum Solo Book	$22.95
00672357	Billy Taylor Collection	$24.95
00673215	McCoy Tyner	$16.95
00672321	Cedar Walton Collection	$19.95
00672519	Kenny Werner Collection	$19.95
00672434	Teddy Wilson Collection	$19.95

SAXOPHONE

00673244	Julian "Cannonball" Adderley Collection	$19.95
00673237	Michael Brecker	$19.95
00672429	Michael Brecker Collection	$19.95
00672351	Brecker Brothers... And All Their Jazz	$19.95
00672447	Best of the Brecker Brothers	$19.95
00672315	Benny Carter Plays Standards	$22.95
00672314	Benny Carter Collection	$22.95
00672394	James Carter Collection	$19.95
00672349	John Coltrane Plays Giant Steps	$19.95
00672529	John Coltrane – Giant Steps	$14.95
00672494	John Coltrane – A Love Supreme	$14.95
00672493	John Coltrane Plays "Coltrane Changes"	$19.95
00672453	John Coltrane Plays Standards	$19.95
00673233	John Coltrane Solos	$22.95
00672328	Paul Desmond Collection	$19.95
00672454	Paul Desmond – Standard Time	$19.95
00672379	Eric Dolphy Collection	$19.95
00672530	Kenny Garrett Collection	$19.95
00699375	Stan Getz	$18.95
00672377	Stan Getz – Bossa Novas	$19.95
00672375	Stan Getz – Standards	$17.95
00673254	Great Tenor Sax Solos	$18.95
00672523	Coleman Hawkins Collection	$19.95
00673252	Joe Henderson – Selections from "Lush Life" & "So Near So Far"	$19.95
00672330	Best of Joe Henderson	$22.95

00673239	Best of Kenny G	$19.95
00673229	Kenny G – Breathless	$19.95
00672462	Kenny G – Classics in the Key of G	$19.95
00672485	Kenny G – Faith: A Holiday Album	$14.95
00672373	Kenny G – The Moment	$19.95
00672516	Kenny G – Paradise	$14.95
00672326	Joe Lovano Collection	$19.95
00672498	Jackie McLean Collection	$19.95
00672372	James Moody Collection – Sax and Flute	$19.95
00672416	Frank Morgan Collection	$19.95
00672539	Gerry Mulligan Collection	$19.95
00672352	Charlie Parker Collection	$19.95
00672444	Sonny Rollins Collection	$19.95
00675000	David Sanborn Collection	$16.95
00672528	Bud Shank Collection	$19.95
00672491	New Best of Wayne Shorter	$19.95
00672455	Lew Tabackin Collection	$19.95
00672334	Stanley Turrentine Collection	$19.95
00672524	Lester Young Collection	$19.95

TROMBONE

00672332	J.J. Johnson Collection	$19.95
00672489	Steve Turré Collection	$19.95

TRUMPET

00672480	Louis Armstrong Collection	$14.95
00672481	Louis Armstrong Plays Standards	$14.95
00672435	Chet Baker Collection	$19.95
00673234	Randy Brecker	$17.95
00672351	Brecker Brothers... And All Their Jazz	$19.95
00672447	Best of the Brecker Brothers	$19.95
00672448	Miles Davis – Originals, Vol. 1	$19.95
00672451	Miles Davis – Originals, Vol. 2	$19.95
00672450	Miles Davis – Standards, Vol. 1	$19.95
00672449	Miles Davis – Standards, Vol. 2	$19.95
00672479	Dizzy Gillespie Collection	$19.95
00673214	Freddie Hubbard	$14.95
00672382	Tom Harrell – Jazz Trumpet	$19.95
00672363	Jazz Trumpet Solos	$9.95
00672506	Chuck Mangione Collection	$19.95
00672525	Arturo Sandoval – Trumpet Evolution	$19.95

Prices and availability subject to change without notice.

0606

HAL·LEONARD INSTRUMENTAL PLAY-ALONG

WITH THESE FANTASTIC BOOK/CD PACKS, INSTRUMENTALISTS CAN PLAY ALONG WITH THEIR FAVORITE SONGS!

BROADWAY'S BEST

15 Broadway favorites arranged for the instrumentalist, including: Always Look on the Bright Side of Life • Any Dream Will Do • Castle on a Cloud • I Whistle a Happy Tune • My Favorite Things • Where Is Love? • and more.

00841974	Flute	$10.95
00841975	Clarinet	$10.95
00841976	Alto Sax	$10.95
00841977	Tenor Sax	$10.95
00841978	Trumpet	$10.95
00841979	Horn	$10.95
00841980	Trombone	$10.95
00841981	Violin	$10.95
00841982	Viola	$10.95
00841983	Cello	$10.95

CHRISTMAS CAROLS

15 favorites from the holidays, including: Deck the Hall • The First Noel • Good King Wenceslas • Hark! the Herald Angels Sing • It Came upon the Midnight Clear • O Christmas Tree • We Three Kings of Orient Are • and more.

00842132	Flute	$10.95
00842133	Clarinet	$10.95
00842134	Alto Sax	$10.95
00842135	Tenor Sax	$10.95
00842136	Trumpet	$10.95
00842137	Horn	$10.95
00842138	Trombone	$10.95
00842139	Violin	$10.95
00842140	Viola	$10.95
00842141	Cello	$10.95

CHRISTMAS FAVORITES

Includes 15 holiday favorites with a play-along CD: Blue Christmas • Caroling, Caroling • The Christmas Song (Chestnuts Roasting on an Open Fire) • Christmas Time Is Here • Do You Hear What I Hear • Here Comes Santa Claus (Right Down Santa Claus Lane) • (There's No Place Like) Home for the Holidays • I Saw Mommy Kissing Santa Claus • Little Saint Nick • Merry Christmas, Darling • O Bambino • Rudolph the Red-Nosed Reindeer • Santa Claus Is Comin' to Town • Snowfall.

00841964	Flute	$10.95
00841965	Clarinet	$10.95
00841966	Alto Sax	$10.95
00841967	Tenor Sax	$10.95
00841968	Trumpet	$10.95
00841969	Horn	$10.95
00841970	Trombone	$10.95
00841971	Violin	$10.95
00841972	Viola	$10.95
00841973	Cello	$10.95

CLASSICAL FAVORITES

15 classic solos for all instrumentalists. Includes: Ave Maria (Schubert) • Blue Danube Waltz (Strauss, Jr.) • Für Elise (Beethoven) • Largo (Handel) • Minuet in G (Bach) • Ode to Joy (Beethoven) • Symphony No. 9 in E Minor ("From the New World"), Second Movement Excerpt (Dvorak) • and more.

00841954	Flute	$10.95
00841955	Clarinet	$10.95
00841956	Alto Sax	$10.95
00841957	Tenor Sax	$10.95
00841958	Trumpet	$10.95
00841959	Horn	$10.95
00841960	Trombone	$10.95
00841961	Violin	$10.95
00841962	Viola	$10.95
00841963	Cello	$10.95

CONTEMPORARY HITS

Play 15 of your pop favorites along with this great folio and full accompaniment CD. Songs include: Accidentally in Love • Calling All Angels • Don't Tell Me • Everything • Fallen • The First Cut Is the Deepest • Here Without You • Hey Ya! • If I Ain't Got You • It's My Life • 100 Years • Take My Breath Away (Love Theme) • This Love • White Flag • You Raise Me Up.

00841924	Flute	$12.95
00841925	Clarinet	$12.95
00841926	Alto Sax	$12.95
00841927	Tenor Sax	$10.95
00841928	Trumpet	$10.95
00841929	Horn	$10.95
00841930	Trombone	$10.95
00841931	Violin	$12.95
00841932	Viola	$12.95
00841933	Cello	$10.95

DISNEY GREATS

Another great play-along collection of 15 Disney favorites, including: Arabian Nights • A Change in Me • Hawaiian Roller Coaster Ride • I'm Still Here (Jim's Theme) • It's a Small World • Look Through My Eyes • Supercalifragilisticexpialidocious • Where the Dream Takes You • Yo Ho (A Pirate's Life for Me) • and more.

00841934	Flute	$12.95
00842078	Oboe	$12.95
00841935	Clarinet	$12.95
00841936	Alto Sax	$12.95
00841937	Tenor Sax	$12.95
00841938	Trumpet	$12.95
00841939	Horn	$12.95
00841940	Trombone	$12.95
00841941	Violin	$12.95
00841942	Viola	$12.95
00841943	Cello	$12.95

ESSENTIAL ROCK

Instrumentalists will love jamming with a play-along CD for 15 top rock classics, including: Aqualung • Brown Eyed Girl • Crocodile Rock • Don't Stop • Free Bird • I Want You to Want Me • La Grange • Low Rider • Maggie May • Walk This Way • and more.

00841944	Flute	$10.95
00841945	Clarinet	$10.95
00841946	Alto Sax	$10.95
00841947	Tenor Sax	$10.95
00841948	Trumpet	$10.95
00841949	Horn	$10.95
00841950	Trombone	$10.95
00841951	Violin	$10.95
00841952	Viola	$10.95
00841953	Cello	$10.95

HIGH SCHOOL MUSICAL

Solo arrangements with CD accompaniment for 9 hits from the wildly popular Disney Channel original movie. Songs include: Bop to the Top • Breaking Free • Get'cha Head in the Game • I Can't Take My Eyes Off of You • Start of Something New • Stick to the Status Quo • We're All in This Together • What I've Been Looking For • When There Was Me and You.

00842121	Flute	$10.95
00842122	Clarinet	$10.95
00842123	Alto Sax	$10.95
00842124	Tenor Sax	$10.95
00842125	Trumpet	$10.95
00842126	Horn	$10.95
00842127	Trombone	$10.95
00842128	Violin	$10.95
00842129	Viola	$10.95
00842130	Cello	$10.95

ANDREW LLOYD WEBBER CLASSICS

12 solos from Webber's greatest shows complete with full band accompaniment on CD. Titles include: As If We Never Said Goodbye • Close Every Door • Don't Cry for Me Argentina • Everything's Alright • Go Go Go Joseph • Gus: The Theatre Cat • Love Changes Everything • The Music of the Night • Our Kind of Love • The Phantom of the Opera • Unexpected Song • Whistle Down the Wind.

00841824	Flute	$14.95
00841825	Oboe	$14.95
00841826	Clarinet	$14.95
00841827	Alto Sax	$14.95
00841828	Tenor Sax	$14.95
00841829	Trumpet	$14.95
00841830	Horn	$14.95
00841831	Trombone	$14.95
00841832	Mallet Percussion	$14.95
00841833	Violin	$14.95
00841834	Viola	$14.95
00841835	Cello	$14.95

MOVIE MUSIC

15 hits from popular movie blockbusters of today, including: And All That Jazz • Come What May • I Am a Man of Constant Sorrow • I Believe I Can Fly • I Walk the Line • Seasons of Love • Theme from Spider Man • and more

00842089	Flute	$10.95
00842090	Clarinet	$10.95
00842091	Alto Sax	$10.95
00842092	Tenor Sax	$10.95
00842093	Trumpet	$10.95
00842094	Horn	$10.95
00842095	Trombone	$10.95
00842096	Violin	$10.95
00842097	Viola	$10.95
00842098	Cello	$10.95

TV FAVORITES

15 TV tunes arranged for instrumentalists, including: The Addams Family Theme • The Brady Bunch • Green Acres Theme • Happy Days • Johnny's Theme • Linus and Lucy • NFL on Fox Theme • Theme from The Simpsons • and more.

00842079	Flute	$10.95
00842080	Clarinet	$10.95
00842081	Alto Sax	$10.95
00842082	Tenor Sax	$10.95
00842083	Trumpet	$10.95
00842084	Horn	$10.95
00842085	Trombone	$10.95
00842086	Violin	$10.95
00842087	Viola	$10.95
00842088	Cello	$10.95

PRICES, CONTENTS AND AVAILABILITY ARE SUBJECT TO CHANGE WITHOUT NOTICE.

SOME PRODUCTS MAY NOT BE AVAILABLE OUTSIDE THE U.S.A.

DISNEY CHARACTERS AND ARTWORK © DISNEY ENTERPRISES, INC.

FOR MORE INFORMATION, SEE YOUR LOCAL MUSIC DEALER, OR WRITE TO:

HAL·LEONARD® CORPORATION

7777 W. BLUEMOUND RD. P.O. BOX 13819 MILWAUKEE, WI 53213

VISIT HAL LEONARD ONLINE AT
WWW.HALLEONARD.COM